Psychopaths and Love

AB Admin

Contents

Dedicated to the readers of the website, Psychopaths and Love. Together, we all help each other. We are not alone.

Introduction

I was the victim of a psychopath. He targeted me and involved me in a false relationship designed to inflict harm. To say I was taken by surprise is an understatement. Like so many others, I had no idea this existed until I was deeply involved in it and began a search for answers.

A few months after it ended I started keeping my blog, PsychopathsandLove.com. I didn't know if anyone would visit, but I just kept writing anyway. As I learned, I wrote, and as I wrote, I learned. And then visitors started coming.

My goal for writing this book is to take the best posts and pages from my blog and organize them in a way that gives a clearer understanding of the experience.

I'm not a psychology professional. I'm simply a woman who has experienced firsthand what I write about. I try as best I can to provide useful information to my readers.

Much of this material is written from the point of view of a female victimized by a male. I realize this happens to people of all genders, so please don't feel excluded by my use of pronouns.

I hope this book is more than just a place to find information. I hope you will also find understanding and learn that you're not alone. And if you don't find it here, may you find it somewhere.

Best wishes to you.

Your greatest enemy will hide in the last place you would ever look.

~ Caesar

WHAT IS A PSYCHOPATH?

LITTLE RED RIDING HOOD.

Psychopaths are social predators, both male and female, who are born without a conscience and without the ability to feel love, compassion, fear or remorse.

Psychopaths experience the lack of these abilities and emotions as indication that they are superior, and they consider us nothing more than prey to be hunted to fulfill their own needs. The psychopath considers life a game to be played and "won" at the expense of others. Inflicting harm, whether it be psychological, spiritual, physical or financial, is acceptable to them.

Self-gratification is the only thing that motivates them and all that they live for.

Psychopaths play their game primarily to fulfill their insatiable desires for power and control. They also play to meet their secondary needs for things like sex, money, prestige, a mother for their children…or even for children to molest. Psychopaths derive great pleasure from their victim's suffering. While this is incomprehensible to normal humans, it's just life as usual for the psychopath.

Psychopaths are pathological liars who will say anything to get what they want.

With traits like these, you'd never expect a psychopath to be charming, but they are sometimes extraordinarily so (with those they are targeting).

Psychopaths wear what's called "the mask of sanity" that hides the truth that lies beneath. The Mask allows them to move through society undetected. They're smooth talkers with a lot to say. They're totally relaxed since they have no fear or anxiety, and this makes others around them relax. Strong social skills are their predatory edge; these skills bring the psychopath into contact with many potential victims, and make these "targets" comfortable and open to contact.

Just when you need your intuition to alert you to danger, it will be disarmed by the psychopath.

Psychopaths aren't able to experience love, and they consider it a weakness that creates vulnerability that they can use to their advantage. These predators gain a victim's trust and love and then involve them in devastating sham relationships that inevitably result in serious harm.

Psychopaths feel contempt for normal human emotions. We show our humanness in the form of true love, insecurity, fear, remorse, trust and anxiety, and they consider these emotions unforgivable weaknesses, vulnerabilities that make us easy targets for manipulation, and deserving of it!

Victims are manipulated into trying to suppress any display of these emotions that disgust the psychopath, but that's not possible. They leak out one way or another, igniting the psychopath's contempt. In other words, there is no way to establish an intimate relationship with a psychopath. He will despise you, guaranteed…but keep using you anyway as long as you have something he wants.

Psychopaths establish a relationship with a target based on a hidden agenda from day one, the only goal being victimization. They are human predators who completely hide their real identities and create a tailor-made persona to gain the trust and love of their victim so they can dominate, control and manipulate them.

They do establish seemingly normal, positive relationships with some people for the purpose of developing a good reputation that covers up their victimization of vulnerable others. Many psychopaths are respected and well-liked members of their community because of this.

Seeing that the psychopath is well-liked makes the victim more trusting, and when or if the victim finds out the truth and comes forward, the psychopath is strongly supported by all those who think he's nice as pie. Meanwhile, the victim gets no support or validation, *by design* — she was probably an unknown, new to the community or in some way a marginalized member, which is why he targeted her in the first place.

The psychopath knows right from wrong, but doesn't care. The psychopath is a cunning and intelligent "intraspecies predator," according to Dr. Robert Hare, psychopathy researcher and author of *Without Conscience.*

If you're targeted and lured into love with a psychopath, you'll be left in ruins while he or she goes on to the next victim. There is no easy way to detect them, but awareness may help.

Psychopaths are cunning and calculating predators. Some go for a vulnerable person who is lonely and/or has experienced multiple life stressors, such as an illness, a death in the family, or unemployment; this is the easy target. Others like more of a challenge. No one is immune. Psychopaths are adept shape-shifters and changelings able to read their prey like a book. They figure out exactly what you need and they cut the master key that disarms all of your defenses.

There are 1 – 2 psychopaths per 100 people in the population, according to estimates. And they get around. One psychopath can wreak havoc on many through serial "romantic" relationships. It doesn't take long for the psychopath to inflict harm, and he can move swiftly and simultaneously among many victims. He can also keep one victim for a long period while having many more on the side. Some maintain a marriage to give the illusion of normalcy. Many psychopaths feast greedily on a banquet of easy targets while taking the time necessary to break down the defenses of more challenging ones.

Psychopaths are notoriously hypersexual and promiscuous; at any one time they may be having sex with their main victim while juggling a few other regulars, having one-night stands with people of either sex, and hiring prostitutes. Psychopaths are most likely to be those who continue to have unprotected sex despite knowing they are HIV positive.

When you've met someone who you believe is your soul mate and the love of your life, it's not usually the time you think of danger or want consider taking things slowly. After all, this is someone you love and trust. But this is exactly when you need to keep your eyes open and think critically about who this person really is and what they really want. Unfortunately, feeling someone is your soul mate is one big red warning flag, because psychopaths are able to so perfectly mirror your needs and desires. This conundrum is precisely why so many jump headfirst and wholeheartedly into relationships with psychopaths. What starts out as heaven will turn into hell.

THE MASK OF THE PSYCHOPATH…AND WHAT LIES BENEATH

The psychopath has only the vaguest sense of identity (if there is any at all), and therefore he has no fixed personality. Instead, he assumes whatever persona will work to get him whatever it is he wants from any given person at any given time.

An identity restricts a person to acting in ways that are in accordance with the characteristics of that identity. For example, if someone is (or at least believes that he is) shy or reserved, he will have a hard time being outgoing in most situations.

Since the psychopath lacks a firm identity, he is totally free from the hindrances an identity confers. Instead of being constrained by believing he a certain way and there's nothing he can do about it -- such as shy, awkward, honest-to-a-fault, self-conscious, too trusting, overly conscientious, prone to depression, unlovable, anxious or whatever – he is free to be fluid and flexible, and he knows it. They have no such beliefs and no such constraints, so they can be however/ whatever/ whomever they need to be at any given moment in order to get what they want.

Marriage counselor Gary Cundiff, MFT, describes how psychopaths use their ability to create a mask to create what victims believe is a "soul mate" relationship. He says that psychopaths select targets based on their best qualities. Then, the predators morph themselves into copies of their targets, so that they appear to be perfect partners.

Cundiff goes on to say that they use each piece of information they gather about us to create a disguise -- a mask --that's carefully constructed to look like just like us, their target. They mirror back to us the best aspects of our personalities, while eliminating the flaws and shortcomings.

"The pathological relationship is a one-dimensional interaction. You fall in love with yourself as presented by this reflecting object." This makes the attraction irresistible, since we are attracted to people who are similar to us. This makes the psychopath highly alluring and causes us give him a high degree of trust.

As a result, Cundiff says, "You experience a sense of oneness like none other." The connection that results is intense and addictive.

When the psychopath wants something, he goes for it. When you want something you often *don't* go for it, because you're restrained by some "way that you are" that you believe you can't overcome. But if there was no "way that you are," you would have the freedom to go for what you want with ease. This is what enables the psychopath to fearlessly pursue what he wants.

Being free of internal constraints gives the psychopath the ability to wear a persona like a mask. The psychopath is an actor and most of the time he is quite skilled, but sometimes things are off just a bit. The facial expression may not be quite right. Maybe he's expressing sorrow, but the corners of his mouth are turned up just a little bit too much. Or maybe he says something that seems for some reason to be rehearsed. But most of the time, they come close enough to fool most of the people most of the time.

It's widely accepted that the psychopath wears a mask. *But just what exactly is underneath it?*

It's much simpler than you could imagine, yet it will make your blood run cold. It's very simple, as a matter of fact. Shockingly, stunningly simple.

But first things first.

Why does the psychopath wear a mask in the first place? Because he has little to no identity? True, that gives him the freedom to be whomever or whatever he wants to be. *But why is he the way he is, and what does he do with it?*

The psychopath is born without the ability to love, without the ability to feel compassion, and without the ability to feel remorse. He is born without a conscience. This is the foundation of miswired neural groundwork that makes possible the predator that the psychopath is.

This basic structure perpetuates a domino effect of other characteristics. First, the psychopath sees as weaknesses the abilities to experience love and remorse. After all, they cause vulnerability and they hold you back from what you truly desire because you are concerned with other people's well-being. But the psychopath, who is ruthless (which means going after what you want with single-minded focus and with no concern for anything or anyone that gets in the way) sees you as a chump who can be easily manipulated.

Because he sees you as weak and he values ruthlessness, he sees himself as superior to you. All psychopaths are narcissists (although not all narcissists are psychopaths; garden-variety narcissists are believed to have an underlying inferiority complex, while the psychopath has no such thing and is not even capable of it).

But it doesn't just end with feeling superior; the psychopath feels his superiority gives him the right to prey on those whom he believes are inferior.

And the domino effect goes further still! Since the psychopath is incapable of bonding with others because he can't feel love or compassion, and since he has no remorse for his bad behavior (even though he is completely aware that what he is doing is wrong), his motivations and goals are completely and wholly different from ours. So different, in fact, that it is hard for us to grasp the psychopath's reality, which is another world we can never truly know. The psychopath's motivations are simply domination and self-gratification. And his goals? To inflict serious harm of some kind, and to gratifying his needs in the process.

Life is a game for the psychopath, and it's one he plays to win. And "win" he will, almost every time, although it's only a win looking through his skewed lens.

Many say the psychopath has no ability to empathize, but he most certainly does. If he didn't know what it was like to be in your shoes he couldn't know what you were thinking or feeling, which is information he needs to know how to manipulate you. But the empathy he feels is known as "cold empathy" – he *understands* what you feel, but he can't *feel* the feeling himself or experience any compassion for it, as someone capable of "warm" empathy would. His "cold" empathy only serves to provide him with information that he can use to victimize you.

So the psychopath wears a mask to hide his true self while he preys on others. But what exactly is under the mask? What is there when there is no persona, no act, and no performance? What lies beneath? Who or what is the "real" psychopath?

To see the psychopath unmasked is to see what he truly is, at his core. It is unmistakable. What it is cannot be accepted or understood and yet at the same time it is immediately identifiable, not at the level of language or the mind, but at the level of the gut. It is a simple primordial knowing that is instantaneous and without doubt.

At his core, all that a psychopath is -- the only thing that he is -- is a predator. *Everything else is the mask. Everything.*

When the mask drops, the person you thought he was disappears. He will look quite different, and any illusion of normalcy will be gone.

You will immediately "know" that he is predator, and nothing more than that. He may also come across as blatantly lecherous. You will experience what it is to be prey.

The moment you realize he is a predator, you'll know that everything else – *everything else*—was merely window dressing, smoke and mirrors, fluff. That was the sheep's clothing, and this is the wolf beneath.

If you're lucky he puts the mask back on, along with the charm that comes with it. But even so, you will never be the same.

PSYCHOPATH AS GIGOLO

The central theme of Don Juan's seductions is not even the sexual enjoyment, but playing the trick.

~Gordon Banks, "Don Juan as Psychopath"

Right after I was caught in the psychopath's web, he made an unsolicited promise:

"I promise you, I'm no gigolo."

Just like most unsolicited promises[1], it was broken.

The psychopath goes for serial sexual partnerships that are exploitative and shallow. Since the psychopath has no ability to love, he isn't looking for a real relationship. And since he has no conscience and can't feel remorse, he thinks nothing of doing whatever it takes to get what he wants. Add to this his charm and complete lack of social anxiety, and what you get is the seducer other men can only dream of being.

When a psychopath spots his sexual target, he has no inhibitions that stop him from approaching her. He isn't worried about what to say or what she'll think of him, so he goes for it; what has he got to lose? Fears that hold normal men back don't even enter the psychopath's mind.

Psychoanalyst Ethel Spector Person writes "The psychopath's insight is always directed toward his internal needs. These needs are not what they appear to be. He is not predominantly hedonistic, although some of his behavior, particularly sexual, might lead one to think so. Instead, he is motivated primarily by the need to dominate and humiliate either the person he is 'taking' or, very often, someone connected to a person with whom he is involved. He may, for instance, seduce a friend's girlfriend."

Dr. Robert Hare, a well-known psychopathy researcher and author of *Without Conscience,* describes psychopaths as **"intraspecies predators** who use charm, manipulation, intimidation, sex and violence to control others and to satisfy their own selfish needs. Lacking in conscience and empathy, they take what they want and do as they please, violating social norms and expectations without guilt or remorse."

Although all of this sounds extremely unattractive, the psychopath can actually be incredibly attractive for the very qualities that make him psychopathic. This is not as contradictory as it sounds. A person whom we sense is not constrained by the same inhibitions, doubts and sensitivities that plague the rest of us can be very attractive. They have an aura of relaxed confidence and freedom, things many of us want but do not have. They are usually great fun to be with because they take risks and seek new experiences and sensations in order to avoid their nemesis, boredom.

Hare says that the psychopath's lack of ability to attach to others and his shallowness of emotions are behind his compulsion to have sex for sex's sake.

Psychopaths are hypersexual and have high numbers of sexual partners. Because they are less inhibited than the rest of us, they seek thrilling and often dangerous sexual situations. The risky sexual behaviors they engage in put them (and you) at risk for sexually transmitted diseases.

When the psychopath's charm doesn't work, he may become sexually coercive. If he is turned down he may get you intoxicated or use physical force to get his way, according to a study at the University of Central Lancashire.

(1 An important note: An unsolicited promise is a promise made when no promise is asked for. It usually means that promise will be broken. For example, an unsolicited "I promise I'll leave you alone after this" commonly means you won't be left alone. "I promise I won't hurt you" usually means that person intends to hurt you. This is from "The Gift of Fear", a book by Gavin De Becker.)

PSYCHOPATH AS CHARMER

"Good Morning Red Riding Hood", said Mr. Wolf.

One mustn't look into the abyss, because there is at the bottom an inexplicable charm which attracts us.

~ Gustave Flaubert

Many psychopaths are extraordinarily charming. But what is charm, and why is the charm of the psychopath so powerful?

Originally a charm was a spell, literally words of an incantation. Then it came to mean an amulet or something worn on the person to ward off evil. From there it became a pretty trinket. It is also an attribute that exerts a fascinating or attractive influence, exciting love or admiration. It is a fascinating quality; *charmingness.* Charming means fascinating; highly pleasing or delightful to the mind or senses.

The psychopath's charm is like a spell, one that's very hard to break. It's a charm that relaxes defenses, allays fear, paralyzes the mind, and induces trance.

What exactly is the source of this charm, and how does it work?

This super-charm is one of the most important tools of the psychopath, one they are able to use very well. The reason they're so good at being charming is their utterly rapt focus on you. It's the focus of a predator on his prey, adorned with a smile. Literally.

The reason the psychopath can focus so powerfully on you is that he's not in his head -- *he's in yours.*

Allow me to explain, if I can.

First, the psychopath has zero distractions, which is extremely unusual. Again, he has the intense focus of a predator on his prey. And unlike a normal person meeting someone new, he's not bothered by things like social anxiety, self-doubt and insecurity. Those things don't exist for him, so they don't get in the way. In other words, the psychopath is not lost in his head like most of us are, thinking thoughts that prevent us from being totally present and prevent us from really connecting with another person. Of course we do connect with others, but It usually takes some time to feel we've connected deeply. But the psychopath is able to create that connection -- actually, the *illusion* of that connection -- quickly, sometimes in just a couple of minutes.

After an encounter with his potent charm, you feel you've met someone you're destined to have a profound relationship with (and you will, but not in the way you imagined). Why is that? It's because the *ONLY* thing on the psychopath's mind is *YOU*. When the psychopath's high-beam of charm is on you, he is *absolutely present*. When that presence is focused on you, it's fascinating. Charming, actually. And we're simply not used to that level of "presence." We're not used to being the subject of such intensely focused attention, and that is very compelling in and of itself. Combined with the psychopath's ability to act in a tailor-made way that's perfect for the victim, the experience becomes mesmerizing.

And because that presence is combined with an intense desire that needs to be gratified, the charm is on another level entirely. As one victim of a psychopath said, "*The sun shines on you, and it's glorious.*" Light is a common theme in descriptions of the psychopath's charm. It's like an entrancing beam of light you can't turn away from, and sometimes the wattage is turned up so high that it's blinding.

Second, when you're talking, the psychopath is *never* busy thinking of what he'll say next. His response depends entirely on listening very closely to you *so he can reply in whatever way that gets him what he wants*. That's the psychopath's only goal in having a conversation with you, if he's targeted you as a victim. The only reason he wants to get to know you is to find out how to manipulate you. He turns on the charm -- which is his generic (but very effective) all-purpose mask -- while he creates the *perfect* mask just for you, the persona that will enable him to get what he wants from you.

What I'm really describing here is pathological lying. Everything the psychopath says is a lie told for the simple purpose of steering you in the direction he wants you to go. If he tells you the truth from time to time, it's only because it will work to steer you in the direction he wants you to go. There's nothing more to it than that. It is pure, unadulterated, manipulation created almost automatically in the psychopath's mind. Why? *Because that's what a psychopath is all about, so there is absolutely nothing else going on in there.*

Many of us learned the hard way that when you knock on the psychopath's door, no one is home. There's a reason for that.

This also explains the psychopath's "sixth sense" ability to read people so well, that uncanny ability he has to easily see who is vulnerable, to know which target will respond to him, to know just the right words to say, to quickly learn your deepest desires so he can pretend to fulfill them, and to learn your deepest fears and insecurities so he can inflict the most damage. The psychopath's sixth sense -- and his charm -- come directly from his abilities to be completely present, to focus completely on his prey, and to have self-gratification as his only goal.

How charming is that?

RED FLAGS OF A PSYCHOPATH

Three things cannot be long hidden: the sun, the moon, and the truth.

~ Buddha

Psychopaths and love are like oil and water — they don't mix. But that doesn't stop them from involving unsuspecting people in false romantic relationships that have devastating consequences.

Spot the early red flags of a psychopath to avoid the serious harm they will inevitably bring to you and your life. None of the signs on the list below can stand on it's own, but together they paint an overall picture that serves as a warning you should heed.

- **He is incredibly charming, in exactly the way that YOU find charming.** Need someone confident, outgoing and warm? The psychopath can do that. Need someone sensitive and a bit bumbling, but with a heart of gold? He can do that, too. This charm causes you — his target — to fall under his spell while he focuses intensely on you. His focus is very pleasing to the mind and senses, and it disables your personal boundaries, your gut instincts and your self-protective behavior *(just when you need them most)*. It induces a trance-like sate — a pleasant, relaxed and focused state of mind that leaves you open to suggestion. You will find yourself wanting to be back in the focus of his potent charm again and again. This superhuman charm is often one of the first and ONLY early red flags of a psychopath, and it is exactly what makes it hard to walk away. This charm stems from the psychopath's ability to be completely present as they focus on you while they figure out what makes you tick, what flattery you long to hear, and what buttons to push. You'll feel like the two of you are the only things in the universe, and that you've finally find someone who appreciates you and understands you and sees the good qualities in you that others overlook too often.

- S/He is very much at ease; he may have a demeanor of being anxiety-free and without any social awkwardness. Absolutely comfortable in his own skin. His ease puts you at ease — you feel comfortable with him, like the two of you have known each other forever. He's not necessarily attention-grabbing or the life of the party, but he is very socially skilled. *May come across as unassuming and soft-spoken while still maintaining a distinct aura of confidence and presence.* Especially watch for someone who exudes a black-leather toughness and a childlike innocence at the same time.

- He's a glib, smooth talker. Never runs out of amusing anecdotes, and can make the most mundane topics seem interesting and entertaining. He does most of the talking most of the time. The purpose of this is to relax you and make you comfortable with him.

- He will quickly divulge personal details and stories about his past and his life. This will create a false sense of intimacy that causes you to reciprocate with details about your own life so it seems like you two are getting close. After all, you've both shared personal things; you've both risked judgement and rejection by being vulnerable, yet you've supported and accepted each other…

- S/He is fun-loving and fun to be with. *Playful.* You have never had so much fun with anyone. You do things you never did before, just little adventures that take you away from the mundane, and you realize how small and boring your life had become, and how stale the world had seemed. You've come back to life, and you didn't even know you needed to. Or maybe you did know it, and now along comes the perfect person to help you do it!

- He claims to be a happy, easy going person, and he sure seems like one. He may tell you nothing gets him down.

Since a psychopath has no conscience and no anxiety it's probably true, but you'll see it in a different way and just be happy you haven't ended up with yet another neurotic mate weighed down by a crapload of emotional baggage.

- He's a very active person who is always on the go. He needs a lot of stimulation and can't tolerate boredom, so he can't stand being alone or sitting still. A psychopath is easily bored, but never boring.

- You feel very special in his presence and feel that he's very special, fascinating and unique, and not like anyone you've known before.

- You find yourself becoming deeply enamored with him very quickly, in a way you haven't previously experienced. You'll attribute this to his specialness and the specialness of the relationship you believe is forming.

- He looks at you in a way no man has before; he keeps his eyes on you and gives you his complete attention. It feels flattering and seductive. You have never before felt so beautiful, handsome or sexy. You feel very good about yourself in his presence. Your insecurities about your attractiveness and likeability vanish as if they never existed.

- You have become intensely physically attracted to him or her, more than you have ever felt with anyone else or even knew was possible.

- If you meet at some sort of a group setting, such as a dance class, he will give you the bulk of his time and attention. You'll feel like the two of you are the only ones in the room.

- S/He showers you with attention and affection. You'll go on frequent romantic dates and spend a lot of time together. You'll get plenty of phone calls, emails and text messages. He'll be kind, considerate and complimentary. You may feel truly "appreciated" by a someone for the first time in your life. It's all positive reinforcement all the time during this early stage. You will not feel neglected in any way at this point. He always has or makes time for you. Although things may seem unusually intense, it will just convince you that this is the best relationship you've ever had and that he is your perfect partner. This stage is known as **love-bombing.** The manipulator will saturate you in as many ways possible with love and adoration, so you don't have a moment to come up for air. There will be many verbal declarations of appreciation and of their feelings about you and all your wonderful qualities, and amazement at all the things you have in common or at how lucky you both are to have found each other. You'll believe it's the best thing that ever happened to you, so you won't even suspect you're being played.

- **He'll divulge his "true" feelings for you very quickly,** telling you he loves you and has never experienced such love and attraction before or that he never thought he'd fall in love again. And lo and behold, that's exactly how you feel!

Your days of unrequited love are finally over. The relationship will feel…*magical.* You're finally experiencing what it means to have found your soul mate, even if you didn't believe that soul mates existed. The manipulator may even tell you he believes you're "soul mates" or say "isn't this magic?" or tell you that you "must have known each other in a past life." You'll feel that you never even knew what love *was* before. You may have only known him for a month, but you're certain you'll be together forever. Believing someone is your soul mate is, unfortunately, one of the biggest red flags of a psychopath. Since they're able to mirror your needs and desires perfectly, they're able create the persona (or mask) of your perfect mate, but it's all an illusion.

If you've gotten this far, there's a good chance the psychopath has already created the strong bond (the psychopathic bond) that is the necessary foundation for the manipulation and abuse that follows. The only thing that can stop it is the awareness of the chance your soul mate might not be who you think he is, and this awareness may help you retain your abilities to see clearly and think critically *if you have been in this situation before.*

Although it appears the psychopath is in love with you and you're experiencing the most romantic time of your life, this isn't the case at all. Psychopaths are incapable of feeling love, and the only thing they want you for is self-gratification.

So how can you tell the difference? It seems like the love story you've been longing for all your life, and actually it's far better than anything you imagined. You probably won't be able to tell the difference unless you've experienced it before. After all, why would you ever think to question something so wonderful? It would never cross your mind to do so, until you become aware of the possibility that all may not be as it appears.

Some things that may help you avoid involvement with a psychopath:

- **Take any new relationship slowly, especially an intense one.** Control the pace, as opposed to letting the other person control it. Know what you want from a relationship so you don't become obliviously sucked into following someone else's agenda (this will help you much more in later stages). *Be leery of someone who gets serious quickly.* How can someone love you deeply and know they want to be with you forever if they barely know you? That's often the mark of superficiality, which is in direct contrast from what it may look like. There is no rush. Time is the only thing that will reveal a person's true character. Time is your friend.

- **Create personal boundaries** and be aware of a person who is able to make you disregard those boundaries, even if you believe you're the one doing it. Boundaries do not isolate you from others — they only protect you from manipulative people who do not respect you or have your best interests at heart. They let the good in while keeping the bad out. If you don't have boundaries, please don't start any new relationships until you get clear on what yours are, and make the decision to firmly enforce them. Psychopaths will push your boundaries as a "test" to see what they can get away with and to lower your defenses, while a good person who is truly interested in you will respect them. Boundaries are not a way to test someone — they are your (sincere) limits as to what you are comfortable with and what you will tolerate. **If you don't understand boundaries, please read a good book on the subject.** A bonus will be finding out what to do about those garden-variety jerks, manipulators and toxic people in your life...and why they're in your life to begin with. Two

- **Know yourself well.** If you don't, a psychopath will know you *better* than you know yourself..which sets you up for trouble. Find out what runs you, process traumas from your past and identify your deepest fears, desires and needs. This is one of the best defenses.

- **Make someone earn your trust...*and then expect them to keep it.*** Being trustworthy is an ongoing thing. Keep in mind that con artists are masters at gaining your trust — that's why they're so effective. Psychopaths are the ultimate cons.

- **Know what you want and need from a relationship,** and don't settle for anything less. If you do find yourself settling for less, you'll know something's definitely wrong.

Delay sex because once you have it, your neurochemistry will shift and you will feel deeper attraction, a craving for your partner and more investment in the relationship. These feelings are due to changes in your neurochemistry that can't be controlled, along with the assumption that an intimate bond has formed. Pacing and slowing down lets you keep control and make clear-headed decisions. It is MUCH easier to see reality and MUCH easier to walk away from someone you haven't yet had sex with. Sex seals the deal. Is delaying sex realistic when you're faced with your soul mate and feeling an intense attraction? I don't know, but I'd like to believe it is.

HOW TO TELL IF YOU'RE BEING MANIPULATED

The more infrequently the crumbs of love are offered, the more hooked you are.
You become conditioned, like a rat in a cage.

Psychopaths are Master Manipulators. They aren't the only ones who manipulate, but manipulation is their strong suit and it is an important sign that you may be involved with one. It's not easy to tell if you're being manipulated...until you know the signs.

***

Manipulation can be so subtle and undercover that it can control you for quite a while before you figure out what's happening, if you ever do. Some manipulators are highly skilled. They're described by some as puppet masters, and you could become an unknowing puppet if you don't know the signs.

As your strings are pulled this way and that, you do just what the puppet master wants you to do. You think you're acting from your own free will, but the truth is you're not. Once the relationship ends, many victims finally see they were under the manipulator's control.

You may suspect something is wrong and you want to know how to tell if you're being manipulated. It's actually easier and more obvious than you might think.

There's a chapter in this book about the techniques of covert emotional manipulation, but the truth is you don't have to know anything at all about the techniques to know if your strings are being pulled. It's good to know what they are, but it's not necessary. All you need to do is look at yourself.

If you're in a relationship and notice a few of the following signs, there's a high probability you're being manipulated:

- Your joy at finding love has turned into the fear of losing it. This is known as the "manipulative shift." You will start feeling stressed at this point.

- Sometimes s/he gives you a lot of attention and love, and sometimes he gives you the cold shoulder for no reason. You're left wondering what you've done wrong.

- Your feelings have gone from happiness and euphoria to anxiety, sadness and even desperation.

- You never feel sure of where you stand with your partner; you feel you're in a constant state of uncertainty and anxiety.

- You feel confused about the relationship and frequently ask your partner what's wrong. He becomes angry or frustrated and he consistently denies responsibility for any problems.

- You feel that you just don't know how to make him happy.

- You may frequently feel angry and resentful toward your partner, yet are not allowed to express it. Communication feels restricted or even forbidden, causing feelings of extreme frustration and even hostility.

- You feel inadequate. You don't feel as good about yourself as you did before the relationship.

- Your emotions and moods are controlled by your partner's words and actions.

- You always feel you're falling short of your partner's expectations.

- You often feel guilty in your relationship and are always looking to repair the damage related to the "trust issues" or some other issue he says you have.

- You feel like you're walking on eggshells around him, carefully controlling your words and actions to keep him from withdrawing his affection again.

- You feel the relationship is a complicated one. When talking to your friends about it, you might find yourself saying "It's hard to explain — it's just really *complicated.*"

- You keep blaming yourself for making your partner pull away from you. Manipulators are very skilled at never being the one to blame for any problem in a relationship.

- You're unhappy in your relationship most of the time…yet you desperately fear losing it.

- You think obsessively about the relationship — you endlessly analyze every aspect of it, every conversation, every incongruity — as you desperately try to "figure it out."

- You always seem to be on the defensive. You find yourself feeling totally misunderstood, so you have to continually explain and defend just about everything. Your partner may say, *"You're really defensive — do you realize that?"*

- Often, you feel irritated and angry.

You might be wondering how you (or anyone else) could stay in a relationship that causes fear, anxiety, depression, self-doubt, frustration and hostility. There are two reasons people stay. First, the relationship got off to an amazing start. He or she seemed like your perfect partner -- your soul mate, probably -- and the honeymoon phase was idyllic. Since you've been manipulated into blaming yourself for the problems, you stick with the relationship and desperately try to repair the damage you think you caused. Also, that wonderful honeymoon phase will re-appear from time to time, just enough to keep you hooked.

Second, "manipulation is an evolving process over time," according to Harriet B. Braiker, PhD., author of "Pulling Your Own Strings." Victims are controlled through a series of promised gains and threatened losses covertly executed through a variety of manipulation tactics. In other words, the manipulation builds over time as the abuser creates uncertainty and doubt by going back and forth from hot to cold, going back and forth from giving you what you desire to taking it away.

COVERT EMOTIONAL MANIPULATION

Always remember, he knows EXACTLY which buttons to push.

Covert emotional manipulation occurs when a person who wants to gain power and control over you uses deceptive and underhanded methods to change your thinking, behavior and perceptions. Emotional manipulation operates under the level of your conscious awareness. Emotional manipulation and abuse lures you in and holds you psychologically captive. Victims usually don't realize what's going on while it's happening.

A skilled emotional manipulator gets you to put your sense of self-worth and emotional well-being into his hands. Once you make that grave mistake, he methodically and continually chips away at your identity and self-esteem until there's little left.

If you feel less strong, less confident, less secure, less intelligent, less sane, or in any other way "less than" anything you were before you met him (or her), you are being covertly emotionally manipulated.

This book is concerned with the most dangerous of manipulators -- psychopaths -- who see themselves as superior and see others as nothing more than prey to be hunted to fulfill their needs. They have no ability to love, no empathy, no guilt or remorse, and no conscience. To the psychopath, life is a "game" of taking power and control and getting what they want, such as sex, money or influence, and attempting to destroy the victim emotionally, psychologically, spiritually or physically in the process. This is nothing more than entertainment to them. When they're bored and filled with contempt for you (e.g. when they've "won the game") they move on to the next victim.

These highly skilled covert manipulators set out from day one with a detailed plan. They are adept at reading you and quickly learn your weaknesses, your strengths, your fears, your dreams and your desires. They won't hesitate to use all of these against you with an arsenal of effective manipulation tactics carefully chosen and personalized just for you. Manipulators hunger for power and control and they will stop at nothing to get them, even if this means harming you.

> "...he relishes seeing her suffer from a combination of jealousy, wounded pride and helpless love." ~ *Abuse Sanctuary*

Just when you believe the magical excitement of a loving relationship has made a welcome and long-awaited appearance in your life, something very different and sinister might actually be in the works. Psychopaths are highly skilled at hiding their real personalities and their real plans. Their goal is to trick you into believing they love you - and they do everything they can to make you believe that during a non-stop phase of romantic magic. This intense bonding stage is created for one reason -- to hook you and make you vulnerable to the manipulation and abuse that will follow.

The purpose of your relationship will change from loving you to demeaning, degrading and exploiting you, confusing you, and diminishing your self-respect, self-worth, and self-esteem while making you question reality. The psychopath will make just enough appearances as the wonderful, loving guy (or gal) you fell in love with to keep you hooked, to keep you blaming yourself for losing the best thing you ever had and to keep you willing to do anything to save the relationship.

You'll accept mere crumbs if that will prove your love. You'll stop wasting time discussing your needs, emotions and fears, which he doesn't care about and considers unacceptable weaknesses. You'll blame yourself for things going wrong, analyzing every word and every mood, going over every conversation, and becoming very confused about what's really going on. Your life, your job, your relationships with others, and your physical and mental health will suffer from his emotional manipulation, which is exactly what he wants. Destroying you is nothing more than entertainment.

He keeps you around until you're the desperate mess he manipulated you into becoming. When that happens, he will announce -- *with feigned or real vitriol, disdain and seething contempt* -- that you bore him and he's done with you, or some other sentiment that conveys disgust. You'll be left an emotional wreck wondering how things went so terribly wrong...wondering how your soul-mate relationship went from heaven-on-earth straight into the bowels of hell.

Victims of this underhanded and deceptive manipulation struggle with feelings of confusion, powerlessness and deep hurt, and many experience more serious after-effects such as obsessive thoughts, lost self-esteem, insomnia, rage, anxiety, fear, the inability to love or trust, use of alcohol or drugs, lack of support, physical illness, and irrational and extreme behavior such as total isolation and withdrawal or even suicide.

The hard truth is that the psychopath never wanted love. You were targeted by a predator for the purpose of victimization, and the plan for your harm was there when he targeted you and found you receptive to his advances. After all is said and done and you're lying alone in the rubble, you realize something was horribly wrong. You will most likely realize it long before that, but will be unable to leave.

When someone starts a relationship pretending to love you but really wants to hurt you, you have been the victim of **emotional rape,** a heinous crime. You will *not* find help in information and support designed for getting over a normal relationship.

How did the most loving and beautiful relationship of your life turn into the worst relationship of your life? The answer is contained in three words*: covert emotional manipulation.*

COVERT EMOTIONAL MANIPULATION
TACTICS

Doubt is your friend, but don't ever doubt yourself. ~Anonymous

Covert emotional manipulation tactics are underhanded methods of control. Emotional manipulation methodically wears down your self worth and self confidence, and damages your trust in your own perceptions. It can make you unwittingly compromise your personal values, which leads to a loss of self-respect and a warped self concept. With your defenses weakened or completely disarmed in this manner, you are left even more vulnerable to further manipulation. **Learn the tactics so you can recognize manipulative behavior.**

- **Positive reinforcement:** Praise, flattery, adoration, attention, affection, gifts, superficial sympathy (crocodile tears), superficial charm, recognition, appreciation, intense sex, and declarations of once-in-a-lifetime love. When these are present continually at the beginning of the relationship with no negative behavior in sight, it's called **"love-bombing,"** and it's designed to hook us deeply and bond us tightly to our abuser.

- **Intermittent reinforcement:** This is a very effective manipulation tactic, one abusers use to great effect. Intermittent reinforcement occurs when your relationship goes from nonstop positive reinforcement to only getting attention, appreciation, praise, adoration, declarations of love, etc. once in a while, on a random basis. This will create a climate of doubt, fear and anxiety, while compelling you to persist. You'll know s/he's withdrawing and you'll fear you're losing him, but he'll deny it. This replays over and over until you're riding an emotional roller coaster, with no way to stop the ride and get off. S/He is doing this *on purpose* to increase his power and control over you and to make you even more desperate for his love. You have become the proverbial lab rat frantically pushing the lever for a randomly dispensed treat. The rat thinks of nothing else, and neither will you. The bond can become even stronger during this phase, believe it or not. It's a well-known psychological phenomenon known as traumatic bonding.

- **Negative reinforcement:** The manipulator stops performing a negative behavior (such as giving you the silent treatment) when you comply with his demands.

- **Not allowing negative emotion:** The victim is typically chastised for emotional behavior. The focus is put on the emotional upset itself, not the cause behind it (which conveniently takes the focus off of him). He refuses to hear what it is she wants to talk about. The only subject is her emotion, which is unacceptable; in fact, it's an issue she needs to work on, and one he finds unattractive. The silent treatment usually follows, which increases her frustration at not being able to express her thoughts and feelings.

- **Indirect aggressive abuse:** Name-calling is direct and obvious, but an underhanded way to make it much less obvious is to drop the angry tone of voice that usually accompanies it, and disguise the insult as teaching, helping, giving advice, or offering solutions. It *appears* to be a sincere attempt to help, but it's actually an attempt to belittle, control and demean you.

- Manipulators share intimate information about themselves, their lives and families early on to create a **false sense of intimacy.** You'll automatically feel obliged or free to respond, and afterward you'll trust him more and feel closer to him. Later, you'll find out most of what he disclosed wasn't true, and that he'll use everything you told him about yourself to manipulate you or hurt you.

- **Triangulation:** This is a common and effective tactic of a psychopath's covert emotional manipulation. The manipulator introduces other women into the relationship in any way he can — by talking about a woman at work, talking about his ex girlfriends, flirting with other women in front of you, or comparing you unfavorably to another woman — just to hurt you, knock you off balance and make you jealous. In a normal relationship, a man will go out of his way to prove he's trustworthy. The manipulator does just the opposite, and he enjoys watching your pain and angst. He is usually grooming his next target, who he conveniently uses to manipulate you devalue you.

- **Blaming the victim:** This tactic is a powerful means of putting the victim on the defense while simultaneously masking the aggressive intent of the abuser. This usually happens when she questions him about something he wants to hide (such as his involvement with another woman). The victim finds herself put in the defensive mode, and she can't win. He tells her that her concerns are rooted in her problem with 'insecurity' or some other flaw and have nothing to do with his behavior or with reality, and that he finds her insecurity very unattractive. Since this is very unpleasant she learns not to question him, and silently puts up with his bad behavior in the future.

- The manipulator will make carefully chosen **insinuating comments to evoke an uncomfortable emotional response** or even several responses at once. He knows your weaknesses and your hot-buttons, and he will enjoy dropping a bomb like this and watching the fallout. If someone says something that has multiple negative meanings and causes negative emotions while leaving you flummoxed and without a meaningful response, you've experienced it.

- **Empty words:** The abuser can turn on the charm and tell you exactly what you want to hear: "I love you," "you're so special to me," "you're so important to me," etc. The problem is they are just words, backed up by nothing. Filling your need for approval, validation, and reassurance with these empty words gives him incredible power over you.

- **Denying/ Invalidating reality:** Invalidating distorts or undermines the victim's perceptions of their world. Invalidating occurs when the abuser refuses or will not acknowledge reality. For example, if the victim confronts the abuser about an incident of name calling, the abuser may insist, "I never said that," "I don't know what you're talking about." The same as gaslighting, really, a tactic which is explained below.

- **Gaslighting:** An especially frustrating manipulation tactic where you know you heard him say something or saw him do something but when you confront him, he simply denies it. It seems obvious enough but if it's repeated often, victims can begin to question their "version" of reality. We also want to believe whatever it was didn't happen, so we may let this absurdity slip by.

- **Minimizing:** The manipulator will tell you you're making a big deal out of nothing or that you're "exaggerating" when you confront him with something he's done.

- **Withholding:** Includes refusing to communicate, refusing to listen, and using emotional and/or physical withdrawal as punishment. This is commonly called **the "silent treatment."**

- **Lying:** It's often difficult to know when someone's lying, but psychopaths are pathological liars who will say anything to get what they want. You may notice they lie so much they can't keep the details straight. If you question them, they will usually revert to denial or victim-blaming.

- **Lies of omission:** A form of lying where a truth is left out if it's not convenient. For example, the manipulator may not tell you s/he is married.

- **Projecting the Blame:** Nothing is ever a psychopath's fault, and he will always find some crafty way to find a scapegoat.

- **Diversion and Evasion:** When you ask the manipulator a question, instead of answering it he may use **diversion** (steering the conversation to another topic) or **evasion** (giving an irrelevant, vague and often rambling response).

- **Selective forgetting:** The manipulator pretends he forgot something important he once said. *If you feel the need to use a tape recorder when speaking with someone, covert emotional manipulation is at play.*

- **Refusing to take responsibility** for his behavior, for the relationship or for your reactions to it. He somehow makes you responsible instead.

- **Attempts to turn the tables and make you look like the abuser:** These skilled manipulators have an arsenal of tactics at their disposal, and they will be pushing as many buttons as possible to get you to lose control. They can inflict so much psychological warfare and make you suppress so much emotion that you can be backed into an emotional corner. When this happens, the intense frustration you feel, but are not allowed to express through normal communication, will cause you to blow up in a reaction of self-defense. *Emotional reactions in self-defense to an abusive situation do not make you an abuser.*

- **Brandishing Anger:** The manipulator will put on an act of intense anger for the purpose of shocking you into submission. This is also called 'Traumatic one-trial learning,' because it will quickly train you to avoid confronting, upsetting or contradicting your abuser.

- **Diminishing and belittling your opinions** and ideas either verbally or non-verbally, by using eye-rolls, scoffs, smug smiles, etc.

- **Putting you on the defensive:** Most of the covert tactics listed here will put you on the defensive, meaning that they cause you to react in a defensive manner. These covert manipulation tactics trigger us to react emotionally instead of responding rationally.

  Trance: This is a very powerful manipulation tool in a psychopath's arsenal, and it is related to charm. The technique of trance induction comes naturally to the psychopath, and he mesmerizes his victim to gain emotional control. Experiences you have during trance states become fixed in the mind and are especially persistent.

STAGES OF THE PSYCHOPATHIC BOND

"I chose you because you were so vulnerable; that's what made it so easy to bond with you so quickly and so deeply."

~ one of the last things the psychopath said to me

"What the psychopath does is they weave a picture of a person that's really a dream. It's a spirit. It's not real. And you feel like you've discovered a soul mate. Once you're in that bond -- and we call it the psychopathic bond -- you don't want to break it."

~ P. Babiak, PhD.

The Psychopathic Bond -- the bond between you and the psychopath -- is a one-way bond created by the psychopath, just for you. This bond binds you tightly to him, but that's all it does; it's not mutual. He creates it to hook you, which is the necessary first step. Many victims report feeling they had found a "soul-mate" relationship...but, unfortunately, it only seemed that way. He creates the illusion of what appears to be a love relationship better than anything you ever even imagined, for one reason -- so he can take it away, and wound you in the process. That's exactly the game he's playing, from day one. And to him it is a game, one he enjoys and one he will win.

These pathological bonds play out in a predictable, methodical way based on a three-part process:

Idealize, Devalue, Discard

When you're targeted by a psychopath and deemed a suitable victim for his game of power, control, self-gratification and entertainment, **Stage One -- The Idealization Stage** -- begins. You think you're entering an exciting, romantic relationship and that you've met the love of your life, your soul mate...but what you're actually entering a sick game that you're guaranteed to lose. The object of the game: He will gain power and control, attempt to destroy you emotionally and spiritually, take what he wants, and leave you a bewildered emotional wreck.

The psychopath lures you with charm, attention, hypnosis and other covert emotional manipulation tactics. He will say anything to get what he wants because he's a pathological liar, and what he wants at this point is to win your love and trust. His loving persona is based completely upon lies. Even so, you'll believe that you're "soul mates" because he's able to present himself as your perfect mate.

The psychopath is not able to bond with another human, but he is good at getting another to bond to him. The whole idealization stage is a sham the psychopath creates intentionally in order to make you vulnerable to the manipulation and abuse that will follow.

He never idealized you as a person; he only idealized you as an object of his desire, one to use and destroy. He was never interested in you; he was only interested in gaining control over you, manipulating you, intentionally harming you and getting what he could from you. As such, his interest was shallow and short-lived, and he moves on to new sources of diversion and pleasure. It's too bad that by the time this happens, you've already pinned your identity, your expectations and your hopes and dreams onto him.

The perfect "honeymoon" stage lasts until the psychopath becomes bored with you (and he'll get bored quickly once he knows you're hooked) and is moving on to new targets. At this point, he has no incentive to hide his true nature any longer, so **Stage Two -- The Devaluation Stage -- begins.**

A theory of "traumatic bonding" by Dutton and Painter elaborates on the idea that powerful emotional attachments are seen to develop from two specific features of abusive relationships: Intermittent good-bad treatment and power imbalances. These are the two stalwarts of a "relationship" with a psychopath. They start here in stage two.

Your happiness at having found this wonderful, magical relationship turns into fear of losing it. You believed you were the center of his life, but you start experiencing anxiety as he seems to be pulling away. You might not notice it right away if the psychopath is skilled at what's known as "dosing," which is giving you just enough attention or validation to keep you on his hook. He begins to change the game to one of giving you just enough positive reinforcement to keep from losing you, while pushing your boundaries further, gradually and steadily devaluing you and taking you lower.

You'll find yourself tolerating continually worsening treatment. But you continue to hang on, desperately trying to figure out a way to get the relationship back to the pure bliss of the idealization stage. He blames you for all the problems in the relationship, so you try to repair the damage you supposedly caused.

You will start to experience cognitive dissonance:

"Cognitive dissonance happens in those cases where there's an unbridgeable contradiction between a dire reality and an increasingly implausible fantasy which, once fully revealed, would be so painful to accept, that you'd rather cling to parts of the fantasy than confront that sad reality and move on." ~ Claudia Moscovici of the blog PsychopathyAwareness

The truth about him comes into your conscious mind, but it's battled by your denial and by his ongoing but intermittent appearances as the man he used to be, the one who loved you so much. All the magic and the passion return when he returns, and your doubts about him are silenced as you become deeply hooked once again.

During the devaluation stage, he will use his arsenal of covert emotional manipulation tactics to keep you under his control, to keep you doubting yourself, and to keep you putting up with his bad behavior and believing his lies.

Because your self-esteem and self-confidence have been damaged due to his manipulation, you believe what he wants you to believe: that you're losing him because of your flaws, such as insecurity, paranoia, and your inability to trust him. You feel you're not enough for him. Your self-worth plummets ever lower, which makes you ever easier to manipulate.

Now comes **Stage Three, when he discards you.** He's gotten everything he wanted from you -- your self-respect, your happiness, your dignity. You may have also lost friends, family, finances and your time and energy as the relationship took over your life. The psychopath is done because there's nothing else to get from you -- he won the game. He moves on, without feeling and without looking back.

"The psychopath discard his ex-lovers with a degree of vitriol and hatred that astonishes his victims and exceeds any boundaries of normality." ~ Psychopathy Awareness

The stages of the psychopathic bond are what describes emotional rape, which is devastating to victims, who may find little understanding or support from those who are close to them. Read on to the next chapter to find out about the aftermath.

EMOTIONAL RAPE

Ours were false relationships from the very beginning in which we were targeted, exploited and betrayed.

~Donna Anderson, LoveFraud

The quote above gets right to the heart of the matter of emotional rape. These were never normal relationships that started with love and then just went wrong. Far from it. The psychopath is a predator who completely hides his true identity and motives as he targets a victim with the intent of seriously harming her. Contrary to what many believe, this is not some scoundrel who wants to use her for sex or anything else. His goals are to dominate her, control her and humiliate her so he can diminish her in every way while he savors watching it unfold. Using her is only secondary.

He only pretends to love her -- and does a convincing job of it -- in order to gain her love and trust, which is what makes carrying out his hidden agenda possible. He gains power and control through manipulation tactics and uses her for whatever he desires without any remorse, while he creates an ever-worsening emotional hell. He is entertained as he watches her trying in vain to save the relationship she truly believed was the best one of her life.

The predator gets bored with her after hooking her, inflicting his intended damage and getting whatever else he wanted, and he needs the thrill of a fresh new victim. The predator ends the relationship with a stunning and completely abnormal display of contempt as his final attempt to harm her. If he is using the relationship to provide an illusion of normalcy to cover for other nefarious activities, he can stick around long-term.

She is devastated as she may come to realize that it was never real and that he purposefully and heartlessly hurt her and used her. If she doesn't realize it -- and many victims don't understand what really happened until years later, if ever -- she blames herself, which makes healing much more difficult or even impossible.

Either way, she is left with a heart, soul and psyche ravaged by the predator.

The aftermath of emotional rape often includes rage, obsessive thoughts, lost self-esteem, fear, anxiety, the inability to love or trust, use of alcohol or drugs, physical illness, and irrational and extreme behavior such as total isolation and withdrawal or even suicide.

A lack of support from friends and family makes things much worse. Some will blame her for choosing to have a relationship with a "jerk," because they don't know or can't believe he was a predator capable of hiding his true identity. Some blame her for staying with him when she knew it was going bad, because they are unaware or unwilling to believe she was controlled like a puppet by his systematic manipulation. Others who fell for the psychopath's charisma and powers of persuasion may blame her for losing a "good catch." Whatever the case, no one realizes how severely traumatized she really is.

The trauma is severe, and the victim should pursue professional psychological help.

"Sadly, some victims of psychopaths attempt suicide as a result of hopelessness, helplessness and the belief there is no way out. Some have reported to us that psychopaths have actually encouraged them to take their own lives or have indicated that they would put them through so much turmoil that their only recourse would be suicide." ~ From *Aftermath: Surviving Psychopathy,* a website founded by Professor of Psychology and psychopathy researcher, David Kosson, Ph.D., to provide help as well as education to those whose lives have been impacted by psychopathic individuals.

Please read "The Emotional Rape Syndrome" by Michael Fox if you suspect that you or someone you know has been through this horrific experience. This book describes emotional rape and its effects in detail, and contains several chapters on how to heal from emotional rape.

FAITH THAT YOU WILL HEAL IS THE KEY TO HEALING

In the darkest hours, you may wonder if you will ever heal from something so awful as having been the victim of a psychopath. The experience might have left you questioning the meaning and purpose of your life, and in life in general.

Where do you go from here?

There are some first steps that can get you started on the road that leads you up and out of the dark place you find yourself in now.

Gaining a clear understanding of what happened is necessary. It's important to have this understanding because when you do, you can begin to stop blaming yourself for the end of the relationship; or if you already know what really happened, then you can stop blaming yourself for having fell for a predator and his manipulation.

There are plenty of resources available to help you to understand. This book -- and the website by the same name -- and others like it that are written by people who have been through the same thing can offer a wealth of information and, just as important, let you know that you're not alone. There are also plenty of websites, books, and articles by experts. I've listed many of these resources in the sidebar of my website, PsychopathsandLove.com.

Another vital part of the foundation of healing is faith. This doesn't mean religious faith; it refers to the belief that you will heal. Having faith that you will heal means that even after all you've been through, you want to heal and you believe that you will, *even if you don't know how that will happen right now.*

It can be hard to muster up this faith just when life seems to make no sense at all after such a painful experience. It can also be hard to realize that contained within this experience is a tremendous opportunity for personal growth, one that may take time to reveal itself. But keeping that in the back of your mind can help you to make sense of things and help you to see the meaning and purpose in your life and in life in general again.

Faith that you will heal is a powerful first step. It's empowering to know that you simply need your own faith in order for the healing process to begin. It's really faith in yourself, and it is still within you even if you fear that you've lost it. Maybe it's been covered over by the psychopath's shovels full of dung, but it's there. Re-claim it as your own. This faith will grow into the determination and focus that will guide you through.

Even if you have no idea how healing is possible, it doesn't matter. You don't need to know right now. You only need to take the first step, which is to believe that it will happen, somehow. In fact, just being WILLING to believe is enough, if that's all you can muster up. It's enough to start the process.

Right now, take a deep breath and feel the faith that you will heal, the faith that is the foundation for that healing.

HEALING IN THE AFTERMATH

The illustration above by Walter Crane depicts Red Riding Hood being rescued from the Big Bad Wolf. I think it's safe to say that for most of us, this isn't going to happen. Once the "relationship" with the psychopath ends, we must rescue ourselves.

We may feel that we have to find our own road to healing because many in our lives (friends, family, therapists) don't understand the devastation we've been through. Even we may not understand at first. We just know we're devastated; we know something happened to us that was out of the ordinary, far beyond a relationship gone bad.

Since what we're dealing with is not the end of a regular relationship, no advice about healing after a breakup will help. We were victimized by predators who only pretended to establish a romantic relationship so they could manipulate and abuse us. But because this *looked* like a romantic relationship from the outside, it's hard for people to see beyond that. Even some victims don't see the truth, and are left believing they lost the love of their lives through some fault of their own.

None of us was "on the lookout for someone as brutal as a psychopath to systematically dismantle" the way we see ourselves, as author Sandra L. Brown put it. We never expected the person who claimed to love us was really out to destroy our self-worth, self-validation and self-esteem through cruel and methodical emotional manipulation. *But that's the true, abbreviated story of what happened, all details aside.* No wonder victims don't get the support they need; this scenario simply isn't comprehensible to a normal person.

What a victim needs is validation. This can be found in forums, websites and books by others who have experienced the same thing, or by mental health professionals who have knowledge and understanding.

In the aftermath, victims describe being unable to trust, feeling extremely vulnerable, experiencing rage, having obsessive thoughts, lost self-esteem, fear, anxiety, the use of alcohol or drugs, physical illness, and irrational and extreme behavior such as total isolation and withdrawal or even suicidal thoughts or actions.

Help is necessary and there **is** help and support out there, but you need to be determined to find it. Recovery is an active process that you need to take part in. In doing so, you demonstrate to yourself that you have faith that you will heal. In believing that you will recover and in knowing that you will find understanding and compassion if you look for it, you become your own source of help and support. In doing so, you will realize the psychopath never really damaged your faith in yourself, your hope for your life or your belief in your self-worth.

Challenges for the victim of a psychopath include:

- Finding help and support;

- Recovering from intense stress;

- Recovering from harm to your psyche, heart and soul;

- Dealing with challenges to your ability to trust others and yourself;

- Experiencing cognitive dissonance, a key element that can stand in the way of healing

- The fact that you're not only dealing with recovery from serious trauma, you're also dealing with the loss of the person you loved. This piece of the puzzle is often neglected or diminished because the psychopath only pretended to love, but it is another important key to healing. The next chapter, "Loss and Grieving," discusses this element of healing.

After the relationship is over, you may appear to be mentally unstable to others due to the emotional and psychological manipulation you endured. A victim can be incorrectly diagnosed as paranoid, delusional, neurotic, or as having borderline personality disorder. In fact, you may have chronic stress disorder or PTSD (post traumatic stress disorder), major depression, panic disorder or an anxiety disorder. It's imperative to get to a licensed counselor who is familiar with abusive relationships.

Resolving cognitive dissonance is vital to healing. Cognitive dissonance is a psychological defense mechanism commonly experienced during and after involvement with a psychopath. It's a form of denial we experience when the truth about something is too painful to comprehend and does not fit into any context we understand or expectation we had.

In cognitive dissonance, we hold two conflicting beliefs at the same time. In our situation with the psychopath, those two beliefs are often as follows:

1.   The psychopath loves me.

2.   The psychopath is deceiving me, manipulating me and harming me.

Cognitive dissonance starts in the devaluation stage, and can last long after the relationship ends. It begins when the psychopath is no longer as interested in you as a victim and so isn't making much of an effort to keep his mask on. His lies, manipulation and abuse start to come to the surface of your consciousness, but it's too painful to take. You still long for the love of the idealization phase, so you go in and out of denial.

Sandra L. Brown, M.A. writes that cognitive dissonance is extremely strong in a psychopath's victim because we've actually had "two different *relationships* with the good/bad dichotomous psychopath." Each relationship required a different belief system, and they do battle within our own psyche as we go back and forth believing one and then the other, over and over again.

We can't stay on the same page about who he or she is, which creates a ping-pong effect in our mind where conflicting thoughts constantly pop up but don't resolve anything. It's as if we were in a relationship with both Dr. Jekyll and Mr. Hyde.

Cognitive dissonance begins to resolve when we finally accept that we were involved in a pathological relationship with a very disordered person, and it can resolve completely when we finally really get that the "good" psychopath was merely a fake persona.

Pursue healing as a goal. Try different things to find what helps you. If something doesn't work, don't give up -- keep trying. As I heard one person say,

"I knew the path back was going to be a difficult one, yet forward I went . . ."

LOSS AND GRIEF

Only people who are capable of loving strongly can also suffer great sorrow.

~ Leo Tolstoy

No matter if you end the relationship or the psychopath discards you, there will be some rough times ahead. That's not surprising since you are going through a serious trauma. Part of that trauma -- and one that takes some victims by surprise -- are the feelings of profound loss and deep grief. This may not happen right away. But as other things resolve and things quiet inside, grief is often what's left standing, waiting for your attention.

This aspect of the trauma seems perplexing. These uncomfortable feelings of loss are often denied, neglected or diminished by the victim, her friends and family, and even her counselor if she has one. After all, you just went through months or years of victimization by a man who never loved you in the first place. How could you be grieving over such an unhealthy relationship with someone who was so terrible? Feelings of guilt and shame set in. But the grief is still there, waiting.

Remember, the psychopath established an intense bond with you during the idealization phase; without that, the manipulation and abuse could never have happened. You may have believed this person was your soul mate, the love of your life. Trying to hold on to that, and seeming to recapture it from time to time, is what made it all possible. Now, the part of you that believed and hoped and dreamed has finally realized there is nothing to try to hold on to anymore, and your feelings of loss can be profound.

Even if it's true that the person you loved wasn't who you thought he was and that the relationship wasn't what you believed it to be, your love was real and so is your loss. Your love and loss deserve and need your acknowledgement, acceptance, compassion, and grief. Grieving is necessary for healing.

Unexpressed grief can leave emotional scars and depression behind. An understanding therapist can be very helpful in this situation if family and friends aren't able to be there for you in an accepting and non-judgmental way.

HOW TO TRUST AGAIN AFTER A RELATIONSHIP WITH A PSYCHOPATH

After involvement with a psychopath, you're probably wondering how you'll ever be able to trust again or even if you should. You found out the hard way that the psychopath was not at all who he or she pretended to be, and that their motives were vastly different from what you believed. After finding out the shocking truth – that you were targeted and victimized by a dangerous manipulator – you might make up your mind to never trust anyone ever again.

But if that's your plan, please think twice.

What kind of a life would that be? You would be cut off from deep, meaningful relationships in an effort to be "safe," but you would still be fearful all the time, not to mention isolated and bitter.

And consider this: If you can't trust anymore and you go on to have your life adversely affected by it, *you remain the psychopath's victim.* He or she is continuing to harm you and your life.

Fortunately, there is another way.

As you learn about what you experienced – and hopefully you're doing that with lots of research and reading, visiting forums to find others in the same boat, writing in a journal and working with a therapist – you'll start to understand that you will go on to trust people in the future, but with some very important differences.

You'll no longer give your trust freely as soon as you meet someone just because they make you feel comfortable. That's not saying you should be *mistrustful* (although certain people and situations call for that), but to be in a place I call **"neutral trust"** when starting any new relationship. Neutral trust means you neither have trust or don't have trust; you're simply watching things unfold so you can determine which is warranted.

I once had a teacher who announced on the first day of class that we were all starting out with an "A" and it was up to us to keep it. The problem was that she now SAW us as "A" students, and it clouded her judgment and impaired her ability to give us the grades we deserved. In the same way, our judgment becomes clouded when we simply give someone our trust and then expect to judge later whether or not they deserve to keep it.

After a relationship with a psychopath ends you may feel a need to withdraw for a period of time due to feelings of vulnerability, of not knowing who to trust, and due to an innate need to become stronger before dealing with new people again. That's OK. An important task now is to develop boundaries.

When you decide what your boundaries are, you'll know in advance what kind of behavior you won't tolerate, how you expect to be treated, and what kind of relationships YOU want to have instead of going along with other people's agendas. None of us decided in advance that the detrimental relationship with the psychopath was just what we had in mind, after all. Starting a relationship with a clear picture of what we want and having boundaries in place meant to protect us can help us avoid the same fate in the future (although I'm not sure it could have prevented our fate in the past; we were victims of predators).

Chances are that in hindsight, the psychopath taught you exactly what your boundaries are. From here, you might also uncover a lot of other things in your past and present relationships that you won't allow anymore.

Once you're clear on your boundaries, *you have to make a commitment to stick to them for this very important reason:* If you're willing to bend your rules for someone, willing to break a promise you made to yourself that would protect you from another relationship with a disordered person, there's a good chance you're having your defenses disarmed. Someone who is trustworthy and truly interested in you will respect your boundaries. When you seem to willingly throw all caution to the wind despite commitment to your boundaries, a large red flag should appear in your path.

The only way to determine if a person is trustworthy is to apply the test of time. There is no shortcut. Remember that con artists are masters at gaining your trust...but they're not so good at keeping it. You already experienced this. Make a person gain your trust and then keep it for a period of time (some say 6 months or even a year) before progressing beyond a platonic friendship. And then continue to make sure they keep your trust for the duration of the relationship. It's not about threatening someone with having to keep your trust; it's about watching behavior (actions) and listening to words and seeing if they go together. Words are cheap, but when you're under the spell of a skilled manipulator, they're everything. But you've been through that before, so make a decision now to do things differently.

Don't let doubts creep in between you and your ability to accurately discern someone's character. And that is exactly what you'll be doing from now on – *looking for real substance* behind the charm and the promises and the declarations of love.

Always remember this basic truth: Actions speak louder than words.

Never let words have more weight than actions. Don't let anyone "explain things away," as you probably did with the psychopath, who was skilled at making you doubt yourself and who had an excuse for everything, even if it was as flimsy as denying what occurred right in front of you.

70

Remember, moving too quickly is a big red flag. No normal man wants to get serious or heaven forbid get married in the first weeks or months of a relationship! Ideally, he might be in love with you but still be sane enough to want and need to get to know you much better before making any kind of commitment, such as marriage or moving in together. You should do the same thing. Ask yourself, "What's the rush?" There is none.

And forget about relying on your gut feelings or intuition (unless they signal something bad; in that case, listen) because a psychopath can and will manipulate your gut instincts, changing them to his advantage.

Become determined to trust again. But at the same time, do it differently: become determined to give your trust only to those who have earned it -- and only as long as can keep it by continuing to be trustworthy.

Learn what might have made you vulnerable to a psychopath, such as desperately wanting a love relationship. It's one of the things that makes a person most likely to be victimized. This does not mean you shouldn't want a relationship – love is a basic human need. But work on losing the "desperate" part, and work on feeling loved even if you're not in a relationship. You always have access to feeling loved when you love yourself. Don't put off loving yourself until you meet some criteria in the future, though. Love yourself right now, because you're already worth it.

I don't believe most people, regardless of what they think, who have never been victimized by a psychopath could see what's coming and prevent it or even nip it in the bud. Just like us, I don't think they'd have much of a chance in the face of such intense manipulation. But guess what – you do now, especially if you've been determined to learn everything you can from your experience and to end up stronger and wiser because of it.

HOW TO HELP A FRIEND WHO WAS VICTIMIZED BY A PSYCHOPATH

We shall be friends to those

heartbroken and in sorrow.

We shall share their sorrow.

~Rumi

When victims reach out to their family and friends after being victimized by a psychopath, many are disappointed by their responses. Deeply disappointed. A victim may have spent months or even years with someone who had no ability to feel love or compassion, and the last thing they need are loved ones who don't seem to feel those emotions either.

People who haven't had the experience of being traumatized by a psychopath simply can't understand it. But they can see that their friend needs support, and support can be offered regardless of whether they understand what happened or not. Unfortunately, support sometimes is tied to understanding, so responses may lack genuineness and originality. Friends and family may offer platitudes and clichés which aren't helpful and can even be hurtful to the victim. Here's an example:

"Why continue to waste precious energy? Why would you give him that satisfaction? It seems to me that you are responsible to yourself for releasing him from your life."

To a victim, these are completely meaningless, empty and cold-hearted words lacking kindness and compassion. In addition, they invalidate the victim's trauma by suggesting she just forget about it, just somehow "release" it like something straight out of Jonathon Livingston Seagull.

Our culture has been so permeated by new-age and pop-psych junk concepts that many people can't think of original things to say during a crisis. Someone hears something, and *ding!* a new-age pop-psych platitude pops out of their mouth without any thought or care behind it, just like a Pop Tart pops out of a toaster, mechanically and devoid of any nourishment. Empty calories, empty words. Junk food for the soul.

So how do you help a friend who was victimized by a psychopath, or anyone else going through any hard time in their life?

Most importantly, *listen*. Really listen, without thinking of what you're going to say. And not just to their words, but to the pain and other emotion within or between their words.

- Resist the temptation to utter *anything* not completely original, such as any type of empty, meaningless and often heartless platitude. Tell them that you understand they're suffering and that you're sorry. If it comes from your heart, it will be very comforting.

- Make an attempt to understand what they've been through. Ask questions, and let them talk about their experience. Even if you can't understand what they've experienced, surely as a friend you can at least connect with the fact that they're in pain and need support and kindness.

- Ask your friend what you can do to support them, and then do it.

- Check on your friend daily, even if they tell you they're OK.

- If your friend is not functioning or is suicidal, find help for them.

And keep this in mind:

"The friend who can be silent with us in a moment of despair or confusion, who can stay with us in an hour of grief and bereavement, who can tolerate not knowing, not curing, not healing, and face with us the reality of our powerlessness, that is a friend who cares."

~Henri Nouwen

You don't need to come up with the perfect thing to say, or with anything that will solve the problem. Your silent, caring presence can ease the pain more than you could ever imagine.

To learn what NOT to say, please learn about the people who psychotherapist Julia Ingram calls "new-age bullies":

"During my 36 years as a psychotherapist, I've seen many clients who have been victims of people like those Hannah and my friend describe. I call them New Age Bullies — those who, sometimes with the best intentions, repeat spiritual movement shibboleths, with little understanding of how hurtful their advice can be. Some of their favorite clichés are:

It happened for a reason.

Nobody can hurt you without your consent.

I wonder why you created this illness (or experience).

There are no accidents.

There are no victims.

There are no mistakes.

A variant of this behavior is found in the self-bullying people who blame themselves for being victims of a crime, accident, or illness and interpret such misfortunes as evidence of their personal defects or spiritual deficiencies."

When a friend is traumatized, make communication meaningful by choosing compassionate words that come from your heart.

TO AVOID A RELATIONSHIP WITH A PSYCHOPATH, KNOW WHAT YOU WANT

When we're imagining our ideal relationship, no one thinks "I want to be in an unhappy relationship with a person who is only out to dominate and humiliate me, and who will use me for sex and entertainment along the way. Ideally, he'll be someone who has no respect for me and who will manipulate me into losing all respect for myself. He must be able to take control of me so he can hurt me deeply and repeatedly, and yet keep me running back for more with just a few kind words or a worn-out promise. I want him to be a pathological liar and I want to be let down in every way. I want to

78

give up all the dreams I ever had for myself in exchange for a few stale crumbs of false affection. I want to be kept on emotional tenterhooks, in constant turmoil as I wonder where I stand with him, what I'm doing wrong, how I can make him happy, where he really is right now, and what will happen tomorrow. I want someone who will waste my time while he abuses me and diminishes me until I don't have the strength to stand up and walk away and I don't even want to. I want to learn to blame myself for all of this. *And I want someone who can make me believe this is love.*"

Even though no one wants this for themselves, it is exactly what happens for many people. How can this be? People are sucked into these relationships by way of charm and manipulation every day, and they are kept in them for many months or many years. Harm will result.

How does this happen, and what can you do about it?

Because of the incredible start the relationship got – the romance, the attraction, the mutual feeling of having found a soul mate -- when things started taking one wrong turn after the next it will already be too late for you to walk away *if you went into the relationship without a clear picture of what you want and the determination to walk away when you're getting something very different.*

That's why it is vital to know what you want before your next relationship begins. Then you'll have a chance of recognizing when you've become involved in something foul, because you'll see it's going off the course **you** charted. You'll have a chance to see it for what it is before your self-worth becomes so damaged that you are willing to stay in a relationship where you have learned to accept being treated very poorly and accepted not having your needs met (the needs to be loved, valued and respected are a few that come to mind).

What are your needs in a relationship, by the way? This is something to clearly and explicitly define for yourself. Make no mistake that your needs are every bit as important as everyone else's. If you don't believe that, you have a people-pleaser mentality and are unconsciously asking to be disrespected and treated like a doormat. Not because you deserve it, but because there are plenty of people who will take advantage of it.

It's also vital to have a strong sense of self-worth and self-respect before your next potential partner comes along. If you don't, those who can sense that will be the ones who take an interest in you. This is a huge issue that far exceeds the scope of this blog post, yet it is contained within it in many ways.

How can you avoid becoming involved in a damaging relationship?

Start by doing some deep thinking and soul-searching and decide on the details of the relationship you want in your life. Describe the other person's personality and traits. Describe how you'll feel in this relationship. Set clear boundaries, and be clear with yourself about why you have boundaries (to protect yourself; to find out a person's character by observing them over time and in different circumstances; to maintain your self-respect; to avoid wasting your time; etc.)

Boundaries include things such as, how much time will you spend with someone when you first meet? Will you maintain your current relationships and activities instead of dropping everything to spend every moment together? How long will you wait to have sex? What behavior is unacceptable to you?

When you can describe in detail the relationship you want in your life and the person you want to have it with and how you will feel in this relationship, and when you know what your boundaries are, you will be less likely to find yourself going along with whatever happens, less likely to get caught up in the other person's agenda without even realizing that you've given up your own.

When you define these things and make a commitment to yourself to honor them, you will then know that giving them up for someone -- making concessions, bending the rules -- is a red flag. Anyone who is truly interested in you and who is trustworthy will respect you for taking care of yourself and will not pressure you to move faster than you are ready to, nor will they walk away because of it.

There still aren't any guarantees, but this can provide some protection.

VULNERABILITY, A BEACON FOR A PSYCHOPATH

LITTLE RED RIDINGHOOD

"Know yourself. Psychopaths are skilled at detecting and ruthlessly exploiting your weak spots. Your best defense is to understand what these spots are, and to be extremely wary of anyone who zeroes in on them."

~ Dr. Robert Hare

Psychopaths can easily spot a vulnerable person. They have an uncanny ability to look at a you and tell if you're a potential victim, one who will easily succumb to their mind games and provide them with what they need.

Vulnerability is defined as being "capable of or susceptible to being wounded or hurt," or "open to moral attack, criticism, temptation, etc."

What makes you vulnerable? What kinds of things let a psychopath know you might be an easy target simply by watching you walk down the street or by having a short interaction with you?

If you're experiencing any of the following in your life, you could be giving off the vibes of a potential victim:

- Loneliness

- Isolation from (or the lack of) good friends and family

- A craving for a love relationship (if you're in this category, you are particularly vulnerable)

- A previous victimization that hasn't been resolved

- A strong need for approval, attention or support

- A poor sense of self-worth, low self-esteem or a lack of self-respect

- Being new in town

- The death of someone close to you

- Loss of a job

- A recent divorce or breakup

- Illness

- Any other stressful event or loss

We're all vulnerable at times, and there's nothing wrong with that. But it's during these times that we need to pay special attention to who is giving us attention. Some periods of vulnerability can be extended, such as when you're single and desiring a relationship; or even ongoing, if you have a chronic sense of low self-worth.

It's sad but true -- the psychopath will hit you when you're down, although he'll act like he's appeared in your life as the perfect person to fulfill your needs and desires. Vulnerable people are the easiest to victimize, and the psychopath can bond with them quickly and deeply with promises of providing something they desperately want.

Stressful life events create a general demeanor of vulnerability -- which the psychopath sees as weakness and neediness -- that reveals itself through mannerisms and subtle signals conveyed by the way you walk, your posture, your facial expressions, the amount of eye contact you make, and the tone of your voice.

What can you do?

When you're going through any kind of hard time in life, when you have some deep need that is unfulfilled, when you're lonely or when you're experiencing anything on the list above, be aware that you're giving off vibes of vulnerability *and be wary of new people who enter your life, especially those who seem offer a solution to your problem or an answer to your prayer. Especially if they seem too good to be true.*

According to Dr. Robert Hare, psychopaths indirectly communicate four basic things to seduce their victims:

- I like who you are.

- I'm just like you.

- Your secrets are safe with me.

- I'm the perfect partner for you.

To the vulnerable person the psychopath seems to be *exactly* what they need, so they happily take the bait. They believe their deepest desires have been fulfilled and their problems have been solved.

Actually, their problems are just beginning.

Psychopaths have a relentless need for self-gratification. They know exactly what your needs are, and they have the ability to put on whatever mask (persona) is necessary to get what they want from you. The psychopath gives you a delicious taste of what you **need,** which gives him great power over you. The realization that he could also take it away gives him even more power, and he plays that hand for all it's worth.

Having needs is normal. For example, as humans we need love. That only becomes a problem when we believe there is only one person who can fulfill that need, one perfect partner who seems like our soul mate, who seems to know exactly what we lack and who seems to provide it so well. That's the hook, the line and the sinker. It's also untrue, but the victim can't see this when caught up close and personal in the psychopath's sticky web of deceit. After the fact, you'll realize there was absolutely no substance to it; you'll see the love the psychopath claimed to feel for you was like a mirage. In the desert, a mirage appears from a distance as a shimmering pool of water, but upon closer investigation you'll find there's not one drop to quench your thirst. It only looked that way.

Psychopaths see human traits that they don't have (love, insecurity, trust, compassion, fear) as weaknesses to exploit. They feel they have a right to victimize vulnerable people because they see them as weak or even worthless. They gain your trust and love only to gain control over you to get what they want.

If you aren't aware your own deepest fears, desires, motivations and needs (and many people aren't), you leave yourself open to the control of a manipulator. By knowing your own vulnerabilities, you can become aware of possible attempts at exploitation. Awareness of your "weak spots" gives you a chance to thwart an attack.

When someone knows you better than you know yourself, you're at great risk. Take the time now to learn your vulnerabilities; it can help you to prevent victimization.

Some good defenses against a destructive relationship with a psychopath are these:

- Know yourself well, which means knowing all the places where you're needy, lacking, wounded and fearful.

and

When the perfect person comes along and fulfills your wishes like a genie from a magic lamp, look closely for the substance behind it, and look closely at the character of the genie. It's hard to think critically and look for problems when you believe you've found someone wonderful, but it is necessary.

MORE TRAITS OF A PSYCHOPATH'S VICTIM

As you read, you'll realize you and probably most others are included somewhere on this list, more than once.

Traits of the psychopath's victim include a **general demeanor of vulnerability,** as discussed in the last chapter. To review, vulnerability can stem from many things including job loss; isolation; moving to a new town; illness; longing for love; long-term stress; loss of a loved one; a strong need for attention and approval; a previous victimization that is unresolved; and not having gotten love, support or validation from your family of origin. Anything that causes anxiety or depression can create vulnerability.

Boredom. When you're bored, you have the desire for excitement. A brand new relationship can relieve boredom quickly, especially one with a psychopath, who seems exciting and different.

Loneliness. If you're lonely, your unmet social and emotional needs create an opening for a psychopath to enter your life. If you're lonely you're probably also bored, which elevates risk. You may have gotten used to feeling like this, so it just seems like life as usual. But a psychopath -- who is very adept at reading people -- will recognize it for what it is, and take advantage of it.

Even traits we normally think of as positive can be used against us by a psychopath.

Are you **extraverted?** This can increase your risk, because extraverted people are easily bored and generally curious.

Do you **"go with the flow?"** This trait could make you more willing to accept the chaos the psychopath creates in your life.

Are you **competitive?** Then you're better able to deal with a psychopath's dominant personality.

Are you **sentimental?** Then you may be more likely to focus on the good memories of a relationship instead of the bad ones.

Are you **sensitive** to other people's feelings? You probably care a lot about what others think of you, and put their feelings ahead of your own.

Are you **relaxed and carefree?** Then you may not see danger in people and situations where a more cautious person might be able to.

Other traits that could put you at risk are being **very trusting, loyal, and committed** to helping others reach their potential.

Awareness of the vulnerabilities and traits that put you at risk is an important part of preventing involvement with a psychopath.

FREEDOM FROM THE PSYCHOPATH

All things human hang by a slender thread; and that which
seemed to stand strong suddenly falls and sinks in ruins

~Ovid

The illusion of the psychopath "standing strong" can't last. Cracks appear in his mask of smoke and mirrors. One day, the psychopath will no longer have any power over you. He will "fall and sink in ruins" when you realize he never really stood strong, that it was all deception. That may be hard to take at first, but with this realization comes freedom.

15321944R00057

Made in the USA
San Bernardino, CA
21 September 2014